CULLINGWORTH

"a glimpse of the past"

volume two

Published

by

Cullingworth History Group

© 2006

Cover design by Norris Hill

Printed by Hart and Clough Print Group
Ezra House West 26 Business Park Cleckheaton
West Yorkshire BD19 4TQ

ISBN: 0-9553054-0-3
       978-0-9553054-0-5

CONTENTS

CONTENTS (continued)

CULLINGWORTH LOCAL HISTORY GROUP - A SUMMARY OF THE GROUP'S ACTIVITIES TO DATE

Following my request for those interested in forming a history group 15 would-be members assembled in the village hall in January 2000 and so the group was born.

Being ambitious we mounted an exhibition in September 2000 in St John's Church rooms and nearly 350 people visited the event and we were congratulated by Ian Dewhirst for our sterling efforts.

Our next undertaking was the production of a 2001 calendar which contained 13 old photographs of the village. A donation from the proceeds was given to Manorlands Hospice, Oxenhope.

In 2002 we again put on an exhibition but due to a greater number of exhibits we used the village hall and for two days, again in September, we entertained over 450 visitors.

Also in this year we published our first book, an eighty page feast of interesting and informative reading. It was available in September and by October we were into the reprint stage. Selling for £4.95 we sent copies to customers in Australia, Canada and many places in the UK where Yorkshire people had settled. *"A glimpse of the past"* as the book was known is still available on special order.

During 2005 we formed a sub section of members interested in Family History and we hold discs of the census for Yorkshire covering 1841, 1851, 1861 and 1871, together with Births and Deaths in England, Scotland and Wales. These are on loan to members at a small charge.

For those readers who are not already members, we hope you enjoy this new volume and will be encouraged to join our group.

Ken Batchelor
Treasurer

FOREWORD

I am delighted to have been asked to write the Foreword for the second publication by Cullingworth History Group of stories relating to the village. In these days of Information Technology, and of looking more towards the future rather than the past it is still nice to have a booklet to read and to treasure, rather than a tape or a disc.

This reminds me of the early days of the History Group, when, inspired by the knowledge that the U.S. Library of Congress is full of recordings of American History, including many Civil War exploits recorded by centenarians who took part, we decided that what was good enough for them was good enough for us. So, full of enthusiasm and armed with a long play tape recorder, a colleague and I went to visit a local lady who had many reminiscences of Cullingworth in the 30s and 40s. We were somewhat surprised to find that the lady was a few years younger than either of us, but she regaled us at length with tales of yesteryear, and of a particularly poignant incident when the Cullingworth Stationmaster's son was killed in a shunting accident whilst playing on the line with a friend. We excused ourselves after a fascinating hour, only to find that one of us (or both of us!) had forgotten to switch on the tape recorder. So much for modern technology, or at least our command of it.

I know you will find the stories in this book equally fascinating and will take pleasure in a compilation of facts and reminiscences of times when life was more leisurely, but often very hard and frugal. It was, indeed, a time when the work ethic was respected and a special community spirit prevailed. Anti-Social Behaviour Orders were unknown things of the future and one of the reasons we take so much pleasure in delving into our past.

Happy reading!

Bryan Hobson
Chairman, Cullingworth Parish Council

A LOCAL FEUD - LANDOWNER VERSUS MILL OWNER

By the mid 1800s Messrs Townend Bros of Cullingworth Mills were enjoying a period of growing prosperity. The quality of their fine worsted yarns had been commended at the Great Exhibition of 1851, and trade had increased as changes in fashion led to a demand for lighter fabrics. The work force had also expanded and by 1866 there were around 1,200 employees, the majority of them at Cullingworth Mills and the rest at their other premises – "the little mill"[1], Woodfield and Ellar Carr. However, in the November of that same year the Townends were defendants in a case at the Chancery Court in London where the plaintiff, W B Ferrand of St Ives, had accused them of polluting the Harden Beck.

W Busfeild-Ferrand [2]

The case had its origins in an incident in August 1864 at the Bingley Tide holiday when, as usual, the mill-owners had flushed out the reservoir at Cullingworth Mills into the nearby stream. Cullingworth (Manywells) Beck eventually joined the Harden Beck, flowing through land belonging to W B Ferrand. He claimed

---

[1] *See Bibliography and notes*
[2] *See Bibliography and notes*

that large amounts of mud from the reservoir had polluted the water, killing many of his fish. The landowner had asked the court for an injunction to restrict the Townends from sending down a larger quantity of waste than had been discharged between 1857, when filtering works were built, and 1862, when the mill had been enlarged. The mill-owners were defending their right to get rid of the refuse in this manner, as they had done for at least 50 years.

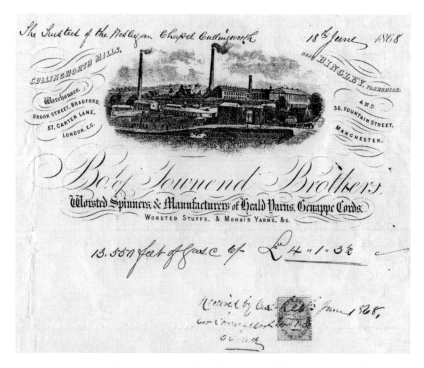

Letterhead impression of Cullingworth Mills in the 1860s

Like many other West Riding landowners William Ferrand was hostile to the rapid growth of the manufacturing industry, and for some years there had been tension between himself and the Townends. When they had taken over Ellar Carr Mill in 1861, a reservoir full of "filthy....offensive refuse" had apparently been flushed into the beck with "disastrous" results for the Harden stream. The mill-owners had assured William Ferrand that this would not happen again and he had accepted £100 for the damage. Although in recent years most of the discharge from Cullingworth Mills had passed through filtering beds, some soapy waste had at times entered the beck. As the business increased so, allegedly, did the pollution and the threat of action by William Ferrand. The cleansing of the reservoir in 1864 had finally triggered-off the legal process and, when eventually the case reached the Chancery Court in 1866, the St Ives landowner was also seeking damages for the loss of purity of the Harden Beck. He argued that it had previously been both a good spawning ground for trout and a supply of pure drinking water for his cattle. The Townends disagreed, claiming that industrial waste from many sources (other mills, tanneries, workshops etc) also entered the Harden Beck. They admitted that in August 1864 the discharge of warm water from the boilers had killed some fish, but only in their Cullingworth Mills reservoir and not in the beck.

A glance at W B Ferrand's diaries for the early 1860s cast some light on the background to his complaints. Despite a busy schedule, both as a Tory MP and a local magistrate, he still found time for sporting activities – hunting, shooting and fishing. Every year he fished the local streams, particularly the Harden Beck, as well as a stretch of the River Aire. There are several brief comments about dirty or polluted water during this period, yet just one reference to large numbers of dead fish – and only in the Wilsden stream. In the spring and summer of 1861, the year of the "disastrous" Ellar Carr incident, William Ferrand was fishing local waters and recording some success, as on April 29 when he bagged "15 beautiful trout". Although there is no specific mention of the condition of the Harden Beck, he must have had some concerns as he called on the Townends on June 28, worried that his cattle had been drinking from polluted waters. Then, on October 11, a diary entry reports: "Gas turned into stream by Townends". This was probably at the Cullingworth Mills site where a large gas plant supplied the village as well as the mill.

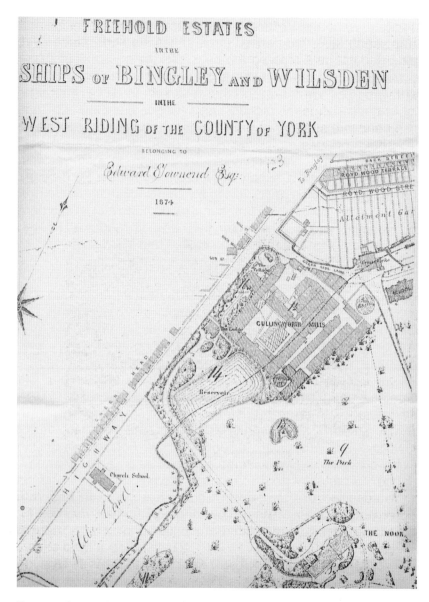

FREEHOLD ESTATES

IN THE

SHIPS OF BINGLEY AND WILSDEN

IN THE

WEST RIDING OF THE COUNTY OF YORK

BELONGING TO

Edward Townend Esq.

1874

Extract of map showing the freehold estate in Cullingworth belonging to Edward Townend 1874 [3]

---

[3] *See Bibliography and notes*

Despite the introduction of byelaws, some manufacturers continued to flush this type of waste (often very toxic) into nearby streams. William Ferrand also knew that others were fouling local waters. A month later he noted soapsuds from a small mill along the riverbank. Yet there is no suggestion that the pollution had any long-term effect on either his sport or the environment. In the spring and late summer of the following year he was still enjoying the fishing, his best catch recorded on March 29 in the Harden Beck. He also continued with his walks along the stream, sometimes taking visitors as far as the Goit Stock waterfall and through the Hallas woods.

Rustic bridge - the Grange

The Harden landowner had less time to spare for much of 1863. There were frequent visits to London on parliamentary business, and in the summer he suffered an attack of the gout, which regularly plagued him. However, he was fishing the local streams again by March 1864, recording a total of 31 trout for 3 days sport in the last week of the month. There are a couple of references to dirty water that season, both on days when William Ferrand caught a number of fish. Although he complained on April 16 that it was too muddy, he had also that day "killed 6 nice trout". But the incident that triggered the court case, the discharge of water from the Cullingworth Mills reservoir in late August of that year,

13

merited only a very brief entry: "Townends turned filth into beck". A couple of months later the mill-owners were again apparently polluting the water with toxic gas waste, but so were others. The Bingley Gas Works were flushing similar waste matter into a stretch of the River Aire, which flowed through the Ferrand estate.

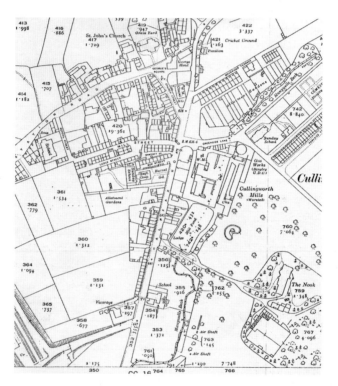

Section of 25 inch 1919 OS map showing Cullingworth Mills

William Ferrand proceeded to take action against the Townends over the cleansing of their reservoir and an order in July 1865, giving rights to both sides, should have settled the matter. The mill-owners were granted the right to flush the reservoir at the Bingley Tide holiday, as they had always done, and at other times as necessary e.g. after flooding or to carry out repairs – but only after giving notice of their intentions to William Ferrand. Unfortunately, as this was only an interim (rather than final) order

14

a decision was taken by the defendants to continue to a formal hearing at the Chancery Court in London. After further arguments and mounting evidence, most of it of little value, both sides were criticised for the delay when the case finally reached the Chancery Court. Here in November 1866 an injunction was granted to restrain the Townends on exactly the same terms as had been agreed before, except that the Cullingworth mill-owners were ordered to pay the costs of the case.

It was clear that the case had dragged on due to mutual anger and resentment. The Townends had been responsible for some of the pollution, but the Harden Beck had several mills along it and drained the refuse from a number of other sources. Also, William Ferrand's diaries suggest that he may have exaggerated the extent of the impurity of the water. Despite the occasional stretch of muddy water he did not appear to avoid the lower part of the beck, which would carry any waste from Cullingworth mills. Only a few weeks before the case was settled he had enjoyed a very successful day's fishing, bagging 10 trout on a stretch between Hallas Lumbs and Harden Grange. After the case relations between the two parties remained difficult. Edward Townend, giving evidence only 3 weeks later for a parliamentary enquiry into the state of the rivers Aire and Calder, continued to defend their cleansing system. He stated that water passing over the filtering beds at Cullingworth Mills came away "as clear as gin" – and there was not 5% of the pollution entering the stream that had done so 30 years ago. Yet by the following September W B Ferrand was recording in his diary that the Townends had killed more of the fish in the stream. Within a few days he had taken others along to inspect the "disgusting state" of the Cullingworth Beck.

Janet Burns

FAIRFAX IN THE FIFTIES

We came to Cullingworth in 1955 when Norman and I married, he from Heckmondwike (the heavy woollen district of Yorkshire) me from Manchester (then centre of the cotton industry). Fairfax Road was, and still is, the "farthest outpost", as regards the village. The houses themselves have an interesting history. Built in 1935 or 1936 by Cullingworth Co-op (part of Bingley CWS) the Society envisaged an estate of rented houses, as a good source of income. However, they proved to be too far out of the village to be convenient: a 1 in 9 hill up to the shops, infrequent bus service, and no one had cars in those days. We owned the only one in the road (which Norman needed for his work as a commercial traveller). Wright Jowett, at number 8, had the only other vehicle, appropriately, a Jowett van. We also had the only telephone, sharing a joint line with number 6 for years. We even declined a single line when the GPO eventually offered us one (there was a long waiting list all over the country). We, and the Welch family, found our "party line" as they were called, a convenient arrangement and the half rental fee was an advantage. We only went onto a single line when Mrs Welch (Nora) died and number 6 changed hands (Arthur had died some years previously, sadly, not long after he retired).

So the Co-op's idea was discontinued, and only 8 houses were built. They had difficulty finding tenants, but then the war came, and some people moved up here from Coventry to escape the bombing. Harold and Edna Stubbs came to number 2 when he was "demobbed" after the war ended. When we came 10 years later, there were still 2 families paying rent to the Co-op, at the princely sum of 9/6d a week (old money, of course!). Later, when the Rent Act was passed, they went up to 15/6d, and later to 25 shillings. No wonder Tom and Hilda Farnworth (number 5) used to grumble that they couldn't get the Co-op to do repairs! (The Government had previously forbidden rent increases to prevent profiteering in the desperate housing shortage).

In 1956, "The Stones" moved next door to us (to number 3). Their name was anglicised; they had escaped from Poland during the

16

war. They had a little girl of 7, Wanda, who soon made friends with Elaine Stubbs, who was of a similar age. Mrs Stone worked at the woollen mill (now dwelling conversions) at Cowhouse Bridge. She told me she could earn good money as a weaver. Edna Stubbs worked at Damens Mill on the evening shift (5 – 9 pm), convenient for mothers with children, then later during the day, for many years.

Wanda was alone next door when the famous cloudburst occurred in June 1956. I heard a great crash and looked out to find it had brought their guttering down and broken a window. Of course, I rushed round and "rescued" her. After that she often came to my house after school. She spent the day with me on Ascension Thursday 1957. As she went to a Catholic School, she had a holiday when no one else did. I took her to Goit Stock, and introduced her to the waterfall. I often went for a walk to Goit Stock with Hilda Farnworth and Spot, their dog. She would say "I'm just going as far as the square chimney field, if you want to come". Incidentally, another great storm swept away the old "clapper" bridge over Goit Stock Beck. It was eventually rebuilt, but not in the old form, a pity.

Wanda by Goit Stock Beck Ascension Day 1957

The Welch's had 4 children, Jacqui, the eldest, was already working at the privately owned small nursery which is now Woodbank, planning to be a Salvation Army officer, which she soon became. Then there was Anthony (who still lives in Cullingworth), Sheila, and Peter, the youngest, only a year or so

17

older than Elaine and Wanda. Cowhouse Farm, then at our back (run by Wilf and Harriet Sutcliffe) had a horse, old and retired, called Kitty, who often used to lie down in the front field. The 3 children, Peter, Elaine and Wanda, used to climb on her back and sit there (all of them in a row!). I often meant to take a photograph of them and very much regret I never did! Then they often finished up on my back doorstep, to hear "Listen with Mother" on the Home Service, 1.45 pm (before Women's Hour at 2.00 pm). "Are you sitting comfortably? Then I'll begin" (some people still quote the phrase!).

Wanda and Kitty 1957

Wilf and Harriet were the parents of George, and grandparents of Harry Sutcliffe who moved with his wife, Linda, and family to the newly-built farm in front of us when the old one was sold for development into private dwellings. This was only about 10 years ago. Before then, it was still a dairy farm run by George and Mary, who had 3 children. Harry, the eldest, always wanted to farm. Robert became export manager at Denholme Velvets, and Margaret a nursing sister at Bradford Royal Infirmary. We had our milk delivered: it was the same milk as produced at the farm, only bottled and processed. If we ran short, we used to pop over the stile with our jugs to the dairy, or if it wasn't yet ready, leave them on the wall with the money - 9d (old pence in those days, and we were always given generous measures). It was interesting watching it being "cooled". There was a device that looked like an old-fashioned metal "rubbing-board", but hollow, with a pipe leading into it at the top and out at the bottom, through which ran cold water. The milk flowed over it into large churns. The water came from a spring; it was good, pure, water and never ran dry, even in a drought. It was several years before the farm and cottages went on the mains supply, not until all the old cottages were given modern conveniences and bathrooms, in fact.

The Stubbs had a pet cat, and Elaine used to dress it up and wheel it about in her doll's pram, an experience they both enjoyed, at least the cat never objected (as far as I know!).

The Ratcliffe's lived at number 1, and they were another family of 4 children, Alec, Jean, Dougie and Peter. Walter, their father, had been porter at Cullingworth station until it closed the year before we came. He still wore his long-sleeved railway uniform jacket for years after. Their youngest child, Peter, was only 6, I think, when we came. He often used to run up the pathway between our garden fences and the farm wall at the back. One very hot day, he ran up, flapping his white T-shirt (to get cool) and announced to me "It's my birthday today!" (as children do). I happened to have three miniature lollipops fastened together with a rubber band, so I went and got them and gave him his impromptu present. His eyes lit up "Oh, a rubber band" he said, "now I can make a catapult"!!

Looking back, they were happy days. No one had much money, but we were a lot more "carefree" in the true sense of the word, especially the children.

Betty Crabtree (still at number 4!)

THOMAS WHITTLE -
FIRST HEADMASTER OF CULLINGWORTH BOARD SCHOOL

When Cullingworth Board School opened on June 3 1880, the headmaster was a young man of only 23 years. Although he had served a 5-year apprenticeship at a board school in Hull, followed by a course at Borough Road Training School in London, Thomas Whittle had relatively little experience as a qualified assistant teacher. Now, as head of the board school at £110 pa he was responsible for around 180 pupils on average (124 in the upper department and 54 infants) and a staff that included two assistants, Emma Brooks and Arthur Lee, and a sewing mistress, Mrs Winscom, in addition to two pupil teachers under instruction, Sarah Hardy and Charles Winscom.

Thomas Whittle's introduction to his Cullingworth pupils was beset by difficulties. Although a new school was under construction, until it was ready staff and children continued to use the old Wesleyan Day School. Many of the pupils were half-time mill workers and showed little respect for either the run-down premises or their young head. Within a day or two of the school opening Mr Whittle had to speak firmly to the scholars about the need to develop good habits, i.e. attending in a clean and tidy state, and taking care with their homework. At times the pupil teachers also seemed disrespectful. As part of his duties Thomas Whittle had to supervise certain teaching sessions. On one occasion when Sarah Hardy should have given a lesson in front of him she managed to leave the school unnoticed. On being sent for, her bad-mannered reply was that she "couldn't come because she had something to do". At the annual examination her work was so poor that the inspector threatened a further reduction in the school's grant if she failed the following year. The loss of grant had resulted from faults in the teaching, discipline and organisation throughout the school. The inspector reported that: "the order is not satisfactory, the children are not obedient and are much inclined to talk and to seek improper assistance. The specimens of needlework were not sufficiently advanced".

The head found it difficult to adjust to the needs of a village school serving a scattered rural population. The catchment area included a number of smaller settlements at Cullingworth Gate, Hewenden, Hallas Bridge and Cowhouses, as well as several outlying farms and isolated cottages. Under the system of "payments by results" a part of a school's grant (approximately 2s 4d per pupil) depended on a good level of attendance, so Mr Whittle was often anxious about the many absentees. The parents of those who lived a fair distance away blamed the bad weather during the winter months, but even in summer there were periods of low attendance. Holidays were not as generous then (pupils remained in school until the annual "Bingley Tide" in August) and many children were kept away to help with haymaking and other farm work. Another local custom was also of some concern to the Cullingworth head. "Great falling off in attendance this week and last", a log book entry noted on July 27th 1883. "The children are employed by the parents to gather some kind of berries growing on the moors". Every year he seemed surprised that so many of his pupils should be kept away from school to go bilberry picking.

Another problem for Thomas Whittle was the number of part-time workers in the upper department. Most were employed at Cullingworth Mills (Messrs Townend Bros) and until now the weekly school fee had been deducted from their wages. However, shortly after the opening of the board school the young workers became responsible for its payment, giving the head "some little trouble on account of half-timers "forgetting" their school fees". It would be 1891 before a Free Education Act removed this burden from teachers. Mr Whittle also resented that the demands of the mill sometimes interfered with the needs of the school. The half-time pupils changed shifts when asked to do so, were often absent from school if the mill closed (for repairs or during times of poor trade) and left early to collect wages. 1884 proved to be a particularly bad year for Cullingworth Mills, with stoppages and periods of short-time working. Numbers at the school fell rapidly as families left the village in the search for employment. When the mill closed temporarily in March many of the half-time pupils were sent to W & H Foster's at Denholme.

Some worried that, if compelled to transfer to Denholme Board School, they would not have made enough attendances at Cullingworth to sit the annual examination and may not be able to leave school for full-time work. Thomas Whittle alerted the Bingley Board to the problem and, after the mill-owners agreed to their remaining at Cullingworth School, he allowed the half-timers to leave at 11.30 am. This meant less time in the classroom, but gave them a break for dinner before the walk to Denholme for the afternoon shift.

Young Board School scholars in the early 1900s

The head did at times show some sympathy towards his working-class pupils. During a school holiday, on hearing that a half-time scholar had been seriously hurt in the mill, he visited the boy's home and later noted in the logbook that "his life is despaired of". Also, he knew how difficult it could be for many poorer parents to provide the items needed for their children's education. A number of workers (some with families) had arrived in the village in the early 1880s due to the construction of the Halifax – Keighley railway, but most would be leaving on its completion in 1884. At the start of the school year in September 1883, when the head was having problems getting his pupils to buy new books, he reflected, "many are justified in not getting them because they will in all probability be leaving the neighbourhood .... there will doubtless be a considerable exodus among the "navvy" population and consequently a number of children will leave the school. These I do not press to get the new books".

Inspectors had often commented on the rough nature of the population in many of the West Riding mill towns and villages. Yet the lively manner in which Thomas Whittle reported the day-to-day events of school life suggest that he kept a sense of humour despite the many pressures. An incident in July 1884 shows how difficult it could be to control his unruly pupils, as well as dealing with their parents. A boy who had been punished for misbehaving ".... on going to his place muttered, quite audibly, sundry vague threats of vengeance". Mr Whittle called him back, gave him four more strokes of the cane and kept him behind after school. The head then recorded with some wit how the boy's father entered the school "..... in high dudgeon and .... proceeded to inform me that he would "thrash me" if I laid hands on his son. He looked exceedingly bellicose and as he weighed about 16 stones his visit had no other charm than that of novelty". The head discovered that other Cullingworth families could be equally troublesome. On another occasion, after punishing a girl – with one slight stroke of the cane and a 20-minute detention – he was "favoured with a visit" from her adoptive mother, Mrs Corley. He described how "This lady in a somewhat high-handed manner and with decidedly threatening mien demanded an explanation of my conduct, informing me that it "was shameful". She further remarked that it was "now twenty minutes to one": but in this last particular her zeal must have somewhat obscured her vision for it was really only twenty-two minutes past twelve". Later, in the street, Mr Whittle was "accosted by the grandmother ..... who probably under the impression that my hearing was deficient, shouted sundry derogatory remarks from which I gathered that it was her firm conviction that I was a hard-hearted wretch ....".

As a result he dismissed the girl and her brothers, choosing to refer the case to the Bingley Board rather than re-admit them.

It was partly this tendency by the head to apply strict punishment that alarmed members of the local board. For some time they had been worried about the use of the cane in schools, and had already banned the pupil teachers and assistants from striking the scholars. Just before the move into new premises in October 1881, following a complaint about the detention of children, the Cullingworth staff had been warned against using harsh treatment. However, it was poor examination results that finally resulted in more severe warnings from the Board. The annual report had in 1883 criticised the lower standards and Thomas Whittle was asked to test the children more often. Despite this there was little progress in some subjects: the following summer 10 out of 12 of the older pupils examined in arithmetic at standard V failed to get a single correct answer. The shorter mornings in school for the Cullingworth half-timers after the closure at the mill may have been partly responsible, but the Board (after several more warnings) issued an ultimatum in 1885. Thomas Whittle would be given a one-year trial period, after which his contract would end unless there was a substantial improvement. Twelve months later the inspector criticised the poor standard of reading and also the many girls, mostly half-timers, who "know very little indeed". Mr Whittle had no option but to hand in his resignation in June 1886 and three months later there was a new head, Mr W Slater. Although he was more efficient and the results were much better, the logbook was certainly duller. Thomas Whittle may have failed his pupils, but he left behind some intriguing glimpses of school life in late 19th century Cullingworth.

Janet Burns

"THISTLE" WEDDING DRESS

The following article was written in May 1994 by Anthea Bickley, former Curator at Bolling Hall Museum. The information for the article came from the Townend file and copyright was granted by her to the Museums Service as she included the research as part of her own work at the time. Permission to reproduce the article has been granted by the Museum Service. If any reader of the article can throw further light on this tantalising subject the Cullingworth History Group would be pleased to hear from them.

The "Thistle" wedding dress was given to Bradford Museums by Mrs Florence Ruth Foster (née Anderton) wife of Colonel Foster of the Queensbury mill-owning family. She had inherited it from her step-mother, Eliza Anderton, née Townend, whose mother, Mary Anne Townend, had been the original wearer.

"Thistle" wedding dress

Eliza Townend was born on 20 November 1836, and baptised by the Reverend Patrick Brontë the following May. She married Frederick William Anderton, of Bolton Royd, Manningham, sometime after 1879 when he was a widower. Florence Ruth, donor of the dress, was bridesmaid to her step-mother.

Mary Anne Townend, of The Nook, Cullingworth, wife of William Edward and mother of Eliza, died at the young age of 21, and was buried (? at Haworth) on 18 December 1837. This was just about a year after Eliza's birth, and it is a fair guess that she died in childbirth, with the baby being still-born or dying at birth.

Mary Anne, unfortunately for us, died before the first national census. This makes information about her rather more difficult to collect. The first one, in 1841, shows William Edward Townend, aged 25, with a daughter Eliza aged 4, and a servant, Hannah Pickles, aged 15. A copy of a family tree, source unknown, in the museum refers to William Edward as having married ".... Pickles of Cullingworth, Shoemaker". This could mean that Mary Anne was a Miss Pickles, and indeed the 1841 census shows a Pickles, Shoemaker, in Cullingworth though the dates do not fit very well. In this case, Hannah Pickles just might have been related to the young Eliza. However, it might also refer to a second marriage, which I do not as yet know anything about! If he did marry again, there were certainly no children from the marriage.

William Edward, and therefore probably also Mary Anne, was a Methodist, along with the rest of his immediate family. The Townends contributed to the Bingley Wesleyan Methodist Centenary Fund in 1839, and William Edward was later Treasurer of the Chapel at Cullingworth. When he died in 1844 he was buried in Cullingworth Methodist Cemetery, even though his name is in the Haworth Burial Register. I do not know when this cemetery was begun - was it early enough for Mary Anne to have been buried there?

We know that Mary Anne was aged 21 when she died in 1837. She must have been born, therefore, between 19 December 1815 and 19 December 1816. Eliza was born in November 1836, and was therefore conceived about February of that year, ie when Mary Anne was 19 or 20. It is likely that her wedding predated Eliza's conception by about nine months rather than a longer period - in a Methodist setting I am ruling out the idea of pre-marital sex! - so this puts the date of the dress at late 1835 to early 1836. I do not think that she would have married much younger than 16 in any case, which gives us an earliest possible date of 1831. Costume specialists who are much more knowledgeable than I am have assessed it at 1832 - 1835.

I have found no trace of this wedding in the Bingley or Haworth or Bradford Marriage Registers. Cullingworth Chapel was not registered for marriages until 1868; I have not checked when marriages began at Bingley Wesleyan Chapel, but it was probably too late for us.

One possible lead is that William Edward was a constant visitor to Paisley. It may be that he married a Scottish girl! There are thistles on the dress, but they were not an unknown decoration on English dresses of the period, so we cannot read too much into it.

Detail from "Thistle" wedding dress showing the thistle motif

The following is a list of members of the Townend family recorded in the Haworth Burial Register:

James	2 November 1847	Aged 53
Stell Wilkinson	16 November 1844	Aged 6 months from Cullingworth; son of James and Sarah, James being Whitesmith in Bingley
William	9 April 1844	Aged 52 from The Nook in Cullingworth
Harriet	1843	Aged 1 from Bradford
Alice	7 November 1843	Aged 82 from Cullingworth
Robert	17 November 1843	Aged 10 from Cullingworth
Samuel	1 June 1843	Aged 39 from Leeds
Sarah Preston	10 December 1837	Aged 10 months from Keighley
Mary Anne	18 December 1837	Aged 21 from The Nook in Cullingworth

Anthea Bickley

HOW DID I GET MIXED UP IN ALL THIS?

Joyce and I were married in 1961 and came to live in Fairfax Road, where we still live, in 1962. I was, like many young people, too busy earning a living to get involved in local affairs, but Joyce soon joined St John's Players (later to become CADS), who were based in the Old Church School in Halifax Road, a building long since demolished. This way of life continued until I joined the Conservative Club in the 1970s, then joined the committee and fairly quickly became Secretary, a position I held for about 12 years. This meant that I came to know most of the membership of around 600 people. This was an interesting and time consuming activity, and I learned quite a lot about the village, and about running a Club, something I now confess I knew very little about to begin with! However, I am a quick learner and soon found my feet. I also became involved with the political side of things through the Conservative Association and started to learn about the ramifications of local politics. Part of this work involves delivering election literature, and I soon found that I knew every nook and cranny and obscure address in Cullingworth.

The next phase in my involvement with village life was in 1988 when the Parish Council was formed. I was not part of the steering group who canvassed and cajoled the authorities to grant Parish Council status to the village, but when they were successful I was asked to stand for election and was duly elected. I was somewhat taken aback at the first meeting to be chosen as chairman - what did I know about parish councils? The answer was "not a lot", but I got on with it, learned from my mistakes and climbed the learning curve. I actually served as Chairman for 14 years, eventually deciding I was no longer really enjoying it and retiring from the Council in 2002. However, I still keep close contact with my former colleagues and help out when needed.

A spin off from the Parish Council was the formation of Cullingworth Paths Association. A group of hands-on volunteers who, in partnership with the Bradford Metropolitan District Council Countryside Service repair and maintain the local footpath and bridleway network. I still work with the group, but the others do not allow the "old man" to do too much!

**Cullingworth Paths Association work party -
I am the one leaning on the shovel!**

During my period as Conservative Club Secretary I became involved in selling Christmas draw tickets for Manorlands hospice, and this led to the formation, some 11 years ago, of a Cullingworth Support Group for Manorlands. Joyce and I run this group with help from a number of other residents, raising about £7,000 each year. This as they say "keeps us out of mischief". Another very interesting period was time spent as a School Governor, first at the old Middle School, where I became Vice Chairman, then as part of the founding governing body setting up the new, very successful Parkside Secondary School. This was a demanding but very satisfying experience for all concerned.

Finally, with my friend Ken Batchelor, I became a founder member of Cullingworth History Group and the Gardening Club.

So dear reader, that's how I got mixed up in all this! If you want a quiet life don't volunteer.

John Brigg

A SHORT HISTORY OF CULLINGWORTH VILLAGE HALL

In the late 1960s keen members of the village community decided to start fund-raising towards the creation of a Village Hall. A small band of enthusiasts formed a committee and set about the task of raising the several thousands of pounds that would be needed to launch the project.

Dances were held in the YMCA in Mill Street and a sponsored walk from Morecambe to Cullingworth, over several days, were just two of the activities undertaken. In 1967 the Cullingworth Old Age Pensioners' Group, now known as the Over 60s, came up with the idea of asking villagers to pay £1 (old money) to have their name embroidered on a tablecloth. Mrs Grace Anderton painstakingly embroidered 508 names of people living in the village. It must have taken her many hours to complete. A photograph of part of the cloth is shown below and a table showing the names is shown on the following pages.

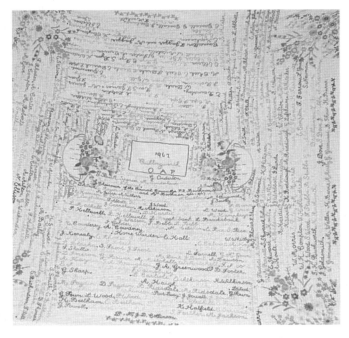

Section of the Over 60s tablecloth embroidered in 1967

31

ABBOTT D	BRITTAIN W	DOWNEY P	HALL E
ABBOTT G	BROADLEY M	DRAKE A	HALL E (HOME WARDEN)
ABBOTT I	BROOKBANK E	DRAKE G	HAMPSHIRE A
ABBOTT J W	BROOKBANK L	DRAKE I	HAMSON J E
ABBOTT L	BROOKE L	DRAKE J	HANSON E
ALLEN C	BROOKSBANK D	DRAKE L	HANSON E I
ALLEN W	BROOKSBANK E	DRAKE M	HARDIE D
ANDERTON A	BROOKSBANK H	DRAKE W	HARDIE J
ANDERTON G	BROOKSBANK L	DRIVER A	HARDIE R
ANDERTON H	BROUGHTON S A	DUNN P	HARRISON A
ASHTON A	BROWN C	DYKES A	HARRISON E
ATKINS R	BURNS H	EARNSHAW A	HARRISON L
ATKINSON B	BUTTERFIELD M	EARNSHAW E	HARTLEY M
ATKINSON D	CAINE S	EARNSHAW J	HARTLEY R
ATKINSON E	CALVERT E	ELLIS A	HARVEY R J
ATKINSON J	CALVERT G	ELLISON B	HATFIELD K
ATKINSON M	CALVERT M	ELLISON E	HAWKSWORTH G
ATKINSON R	CARLISLE J	ELLISON H	HAWKSWORTH S
BAILEY C	CARLISLE L	ELLISON N	HAYNES A
BAILEY E	CARTER	ELLISON R	HEATON E
BAILEY I	CARTER A	ELLISON R E	HELLEWELL L
BAILEY J I	CARTER E	FARNELL L	HELLEWELL P
BAILEY M	CHALK L	FARNELL R	HEY A
BAIRD DR	CHALK N	FARNWORTH I	HEYWARD C
BAIRD MR & MRS	CHAPMAN A	FARROW F	HEYWOOD E
BALDWIN A	CHEEK E	FARROW H	HILLERY J
BALDWIN E	CHEEK M	FARROW T	HILLERY M
BALDWIN L	CHILTON E	FEATHER S	HINCHCLIFFE H
BALDWIN M	CHILTON W	FOSTER B	HINCHLIFFE J
BALDWIN N	CLATON C	FOSTER S L	HIRD B
BANCROFT G	CLAYTON H	FOSTER W	HIRD J
BARKER E	COATES G	FROST H	HITCHIN E
BARKER H	COLE A	FROST J	HITHCIN M
BARRACLOUGH E	COLLEDGE ?	FROST S	HITCHIN N
BARRACLOUGH I	COLLINSON JD & MRS	GELDER I	HITCHIN W
BARTLE L S	COMPTON A	GIBBON C	HOBSON I
BEARDS A	COMPTON E	GIBBONS H	HOLLINDRAKE A
BEARDS L	COMPTON H	GIBBONS C	HOLLINDRAKE G
BEARDS N	COMPTON J	GIBBONS H	HOLLINDRAKE V
BEBB J	COMPTON M	GIBBONS ?	HOLLINGS I
BEBB L	COMPTON W H	GIBSON ?	HOLLINGSWORTH E
BEETHAM H	COPE M	GIBSON D	HOLLINGSWORTH G
BEETHAM M	COPE N	GILL I	HOPKINSON
BEETHAN E	COPE P	GILL J	HOPKINSON B
BINNS M	COPE R	GILL W	HOPKINSON E
BIRD J	COPLAND I	GILSON D	HOPKINSON V
BLACKA A	COPLAND J	GLEDHIILL A	HOULT E
BLACKA E	COWDEREY A	GLOVER M	HOULT H
BLACKA I	COWDEREY R	GOLDSMITH A	HOWARTH M
BLACKA J	COWGILL A	GOLDSMITH J	HOYLE M
BLACKA L	CRABTREE E	GOODALL	HUDSON B
BLACKA M	CRAVEN A	GOODALL E	HUDSON H
BLACKA S H	CRAVEN C	GOODALL G	HUDSON J
BLACKA W	CRIDLAND N	GOVE L	HUDSON V
BOARDMAN F	DAVIDSON E	GOVE M	HULATT C
BOARDMAN M	DAVIDSON N	GREAVES M	HULLATT F
BOOTH L	DAWSON A	GREAVES W	HUMPHREYS C
BOOTH PR COUNCILLOR	DENT J	GREEN G H	HUMPHREYS H
MRS BOOTHMAN	DENT M	GREEN H G	HUMPHREYS M
BOWER A	DERRICK B	GREEN J	HURRY E
BOWER G	DERRICK E	GREEN J A	IBBE E
BOYES K	DOLPHIN W	GREENIO? E	ILLINGSWORTH M
BREATON J	DOVE H	GREENWOOD E	IMESON D
BREATON M	DOVE J	GREENWOOD G	JACKSON I
BRETT A	DOVE L	GREENWOOD J A (JP)	JACKSON J
BRIGG J	DOVE S	GREENWOOD W	JACKSON M
BRIGGS E	DOWNEY G	GREY I	JAGGER J AND MRS (CLLR)
BRITTAIN B	DOWNEY J	HAIGH A	JAGGER MR & MRS

JAMES MRS	PEACOCK M	SHACKLETON S	THOMAS L
JAMES S I (REV &	PEACOCK N	SHALLIS F	THOMAS L
MRS JAMES)	PEACOCK O	SHARP A	THOMAS W
JESSOP M	PHILIPSON L	SHARP G	THOMPSON D
JONES S	PHILIPSON S	SHAW B	THOMPSON V
JOWETT E	PHILLIPS L	SHAW L	THROUP M
JOWETT I	PICKLES M E	SHIMM G	TIDSWELL D
JOWETT J	PINDER D & R H	SHWARCK E	TIFFANY A
JOWETT J (POST	POVEY L	SHWARCK S	TIFFANY D
LADY)	POWELL G	SIMPSON	TIFFANY J
KELLY E	POWELL M	SIMPSON H	TIFFANY S
KENEAK W	POWIS D	SIMPSON J	TOLL C
KENEALY J	PRESTON A	SIMPSON M	TOLL T
KENEALY W	RANDALL E M	SIMPSON R	TOLL V
KENWORTH H	RAWNSLEY A	SLATER C	TOMLINSON A
KENWORTHY A	RAWNSLEY E	SLATER C C	TOMLINSON W
KENWORTHY C	RAYNOR E	SLATER V	TOWN G
LAMBERT A	REDDIOUGH A	SMITH A	TOWNEND E
LLOYD D	REDDIOUGH K	SMITH A L	WAITES A
LLOYD N	REDDIOUGH M	SMITH C	WALKER M
LOFTHOUSE G	REDMAN F	SMITH E	WASHINGTON E
LOFTHOUSE G	REDMAN I	SMITH I	WATSON M
LONGBOTTOM M	RHODES B	SMITH J	WEBB A
LUND E	RHODES E	SMITH L	WEBSTER M
LUND J	RHODES J	SMITH M	WHITAKER A
LUND R	RHODES M	SMITH N	WHITAKER E
LYON H	RHODES M J	SMITH S	WHITAKER H
LYON S	RHODES R	SNOWDEN H	WHITAKER H
MACHELL J	RICE E	SNOWDEN M	WHITAKER L
MACHELL L	RICE S	SPENCER B	WHITAKER M
MACHELL M	RICHARDSON E	SPENCER E	WHITAKER N
MALTBY H	RIDSDALE B	SPENCER M	WHITAKER S
McGOWN G	RIDSDALE M	SPENCER P	WHITBY H
MEAKIN E	RILEY E	STAFFORD	WHITBY W
MILES L	ROBERTS L	STAFFORD J G V M	WHITWHAM A
MILLWARD A	ROBERTS M	STEIN A	WHITWHAM K
MINNIKIN J W	ROBINSON S	STEWART E	WHITWHAM M
MITCHELL E	ROBINSON B	STEWART R	WICKENDEN G
MITCHELL M	ROBINSON J	STITSON E	WILKINSON A
MITCHELL W	ROBINSON J E	STITSON H	WILKINSON C P
MOLES A	ROBINSON S	STITSON S	WILKINSON H
MOORE F	RUSHWORTH T H	STOREY M	WILKINSON L
MOORE T	RYDER B	STUBBS A	WILKINSON W
MORRIS M	RYE G	STUBBS B	WILLIAMSON D
MORRIS W	SAINSBURY E S	STUBBS E	WILSON I
MURRAY J	SAINSBURY G	STUBBS H	WILSON T
NELSON E	SAINSBURY J	STUBBS J	WINDLE H
NEWMAN S	SAMPSON H	STUBBS L	WOOD D
NORMING J K	SAMPSON K	STUBBS W	WOOD E
PAGDIN D	SAWLEY J	SUCKLEY J	WOOD G
PAGDIN M	SCOTT H	SUMERVILLE ?	WOOD J
PALMER E	SCOTT I	SUNDERLAND C	WOOD L
PARRATT A	SCOTT T	SUNDERLAND M	WOOD P
PARRATT A (DR)	SERRANT C	SUNDERLAND W	WOOD S
PARRATT K	SHACKLETON E	SUTHERS A	WOODS J
PASSMAN N	SHACKLETON G	THEOBALD G	WRACK M N
PASSMAN R	SHACKLETON I	THOMAS D	WYNNE D
PEACOCK E	SHACKLETON J	THOMAS E	WYNNE J

Over 60s Club Table Cloth Names List 1967 [1]

---

[1] See Bibliography and notes

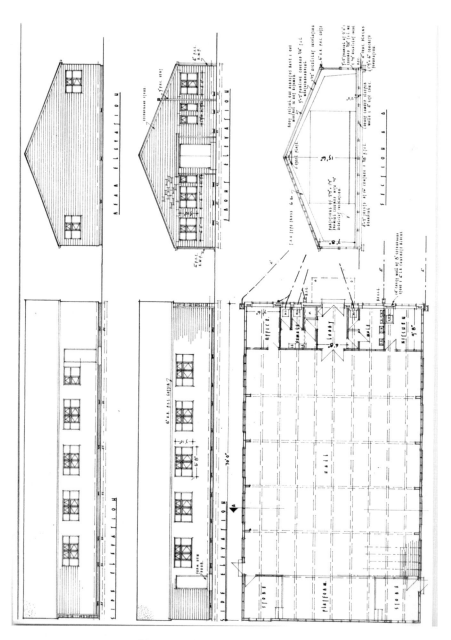

Plans of the original building

Eventually a suitable building became available in Keighley, standing on the site of the present Damside Car Park. It was the redundant Salvation Army Citadel Hall and following negotiations was purchased for the sum of £2,000.

A site needed to be found for the erection of the building and the clearance of the cottages in Coronation Street and Francis Square provided the opportunity for the scheme to progress. People have since remarked that the houses were prematurely demolished, as with careful modification they could have been saved as affordable housing in the village. The properties could have been completely renovated to become a desirable feature in the conservation area. However, it was the fashion then to destroy many sound buildings, a policy we have lived to regret.

In the early days the hall was used to provide entertainment for the villagers in a period when the simple pleasures were much appreciated. Whist drives, bingo sessions, dances and a youth club were the activities taking place under the care of the trustees. In the original constitution, drawn up with Bradford Local Council, the owners of the land, the trustees numbered 26. The land is leased to the Hall Management Committee at a peppercorn rent.

In the early days a play school operated in the hall staffed by parents which gave a start to toddlers and was much appreciated. Since those days a Pre-School has been in existence for many years and is regularly inspected by "OFSTED". It is open morning and afternoons Monday, Tuesday, Wednesday and Friday, with mornings only on Thursdays. The Over 60s Club meets on Thursday afternoons, when a programme of entertainment is provided for the older members of the village.

A long established activity is the Cullingworth Amateur Dramatic Society (CADS). The group started life as The St Johns Players before the war, meeting in those days in the Sunday School building (now demolished) in Halifax Road opposite the Vicarage. The change of name came about in the late 1960s and following the opening of the Village Hall in 1973, the first show presented was "Cat among the Pigeons". CADS is still very active putting on various plays, musicals and pantomimes.

When the hall was first built its emblem was a white elephant, and it was the opinion of a lot of villagers that it would become a "white elephant". However, over the years it has been well used and with a constant repair and maintenance programme is still in good shape.

Official Opening Saturday 6 April 1974
Mrs Janet Whitehead, Mrs Pam Price, Mrs Betty Crabtree, Mr Frank Jagger,
Chairman, Mrs P Clayton, Mrs Stella Ward, Mrs Terry Stammers, Mr
Maurice Bennett, Mrs Margaret Bennett, Janet Wilkinson, Mrs B Smith, Mrs
Barbara Thompson, Secretary, Mr Harry Lobley, Mr W Minniken, Mrs
Downey, Councillor Mrs Emily Hall, Official opener Last Chairman of
Bingley Urban District Council before it was taken over by Bradford
Metropolitan District Council, Lynne Bennett, Barbara Slater

The photograph on the previous page shows the gathering of the people most involved in the venture and it is nice to realise that some are still active in the hall scene today, some 30 years later.

A grant from the EEC was used to extend the front to provide a committee room, toilets and storeroom and recently a ramp was installed to provide access for disabled users.

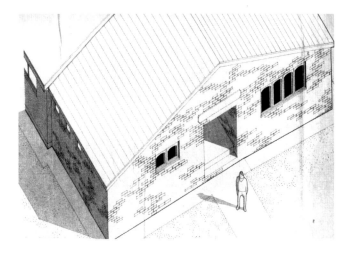

Isometric projection of extension mid 1980s

If only it were possible to raise the necessary funding to rebuild in stone this would enhance the centre of the village and could provide several small rooms for small groups, together with a large hall capable of being divided if required.

The original cost of the hall was a struggle to raise but it would go nowhere in providing a replacement today!

Thanks must go to everyone involved over the years in keeping the project alive and particularly to the present Chairman, Ralph Beards, who has guided the management over the last 7 years.

Ken Batchelor

MEMORIES OF THE BAPTIST CHAPEL

The Baptist Chapel was a very busy place. There was a badminton court, where matches were played. This was very popular and they had a very successful team.

Early exterior of the Baptist Chapel

It was also the venue for fancy dress parties, pantomimes, plays and also an old time music hall. The concert party was known as The Cheer Uptomists and one of their songs went as follows:

> At old Cullingworth by the moor
> We've heard you've got a new bus station
> The buses bounce up Mill Street
> Then go in for repair
> There was one in Passman's Cellar
> With its front wheels in the air
> They've even taken your shelter now
> So that you can have fresh air
> At old Cullingworth by the moor.

This was sung to the *"Much Binding in the Marsh"* tune. The reference to Passman's Cellar refers to Renny Passman's butcher's shop, (now Paul Ellison's butcher's shop). There were more verses but unfortunately I am unable to remember them.

The accompanist was Mr Wilfred Greaves, who was assisted by his wife who was also a very able pianist.

The comics were played by Alan Towler and Harry Gibson.

The Chapel even had an orchestra and put on operettas and also performed the *"Messiah"*.

Interior of the Baptist Chapel

The acoustics in the actual Chapel were superb, as was the organ. Bob Andrews who used to be the organist at Bingley Parish Church said he always enjoyed playing it.

Janet Wharton

REMINISCENCES OF LIFE IN CULLINGWORTH BEFORE 1955

I was born and spent my first two years in a house called Holmlea, which was next to my father, James Hollings, butcher's shop on Halifax Road, Cullingworth. Our family then moved to Rock House near the Station in Station Road Cullingworth but we still owned the butcher's shop, which has over the years been various types of shop and is now a hairdressers. And when I was very young, grandfather, Walter Hollings, had a wooden butcher's shop at the bottom of Sun Street.

GRANDFATHER'S
BUTCHERS SHOP, SUN ST. 1910ᵗʰ Brenda Watering'04.

Grandfather's butcher's shop Sun Street 1910

40

As I grew up I spent time calling in to see how Dad was getting on in his butcher's shop, coming eye to cow's eye on the slab. Locals would come in to have a cheerful chat with Dad, who was always a happy person. They would pat my curly blonde head and say how I was getting a "bigger little girl" - but not big enough for me as my friend was a fraction taller and what's more her feet were bigger than mine - this made all the difference to a five or six year old!

At Christmas, so my brother Kenneth tells me, Dad had a little Father Christmas mechanically moving a little fishing line around which tapped gently on the shop window for all to watch.

As the working day drew to a close and father cleaned the shop and his equipment, I was sometimes allowed to play with his sausage maker before it was washed - complete magic, better than any toy!

Opposite the shop was a very special gents' toilet - a decorative iron one. I used to watch men walk in one end, their feet visible as they disappeared inside. All to be watched without even leaving the shop window!

Getting up in the morning at Rock House to the beautiful open views across the four fields; my mother's favourite pink blossom tree down the field heralded spring and summer holidays soon.

My friends and I used to roly poly down the four fields opposite Rock House - no new houses then only open fields - and of course rolled through various cow pats. We climbed small trees and ripped our clothing but thoroughly enjoyed ourselves.

We would wander down the four fields through the woody bit called Ellar Carr, where John Ambler Greenwood had a house on a huge rocky area with water around it like a moat below. The air would be filled with the sound of insects and the nearby field had a lovely running stream, with tadpoles and frogs and dragonflies. We paddled here and I lay on the sloping field in the sun.

ROCK HOUSE
IN 1940

Brenda Watering '04

Rock House 1940

When at the Board School we used to be taken by Miss Johns to a garden near Barry Greenwood's house, probably part of his garden which was also near the house on the rock. Miss Johns had several bee hives here and we donned big veiled hats and gloves, and the combs full of honey were examined.

I was a shy little girl on my first day at the Board School, hoping mum would pick me up soon. Another little child was allocated to look after new pupils on arrival - mine was Pauline Barker. She had a pretty silky check apron on. I was very happy at the School. Miss Pickles was great at reading "Larry the Lamb" with appropriate noises. Miss Johns always wore pale colours which I thought delightful especially if fluffy, and Miss Goodyear kept us all in order. Mr Baker was our headmaster.

Each morning a Klaxon would go off in the village and also when the mill was closed later in the day. This was Cravens Mill - only the imposing gate remains today, by the cenotaph. Mr Craven was a smart man with a silver topped cane, and his wife always had a kind soft voice. They lived in a splendid house with turrets, called Hallas Hall, now demolished and replaced with Ainsdale Grove. It had a narrow gauge railway which went round the garden.

More or less from birth my first friend was Janet Wharton (née Towler). Janet lived in one of the three houses called Moorlands, the next block to Rock House - there was a block of four houses built about 1870. Rock House was the top one, and Janet's the bottom of the other three. We used to visit and play together, then Janet moved to The Nook, a lovely old house where I and many friends enjoyed ourselves, sometimes dressing up in Cavalier capes and hats, marching through the woods there. Summertime came and a village fete was held on The Nook lawns with trestle tables full of goodies, knitted garments, cakes and of course teas and lemonade. It was wonderful. That's where I bought some baby bootees for my doll. A boy, I can't remember who, asked if I would exchange them for his smaller pair, bought for the family new baby. I preferred to hang on to them for my doll - I feel guilty to this day!

The old house was lovely.   A part much older than the rest contained the morning room,   with a huge old stone fireplace, a fire blazing in the hearth, and the kitchen full of old cupboards and a big dresser.

THE NOOK
EAST VIEW

Brenda Watering 2004

The Nook - east view

We children used to climb the lovely little staircase to the attic where Janet's brother had his train set permanently out and we used to play with it.

Mollie Pepper (née Suthers) came to live in the middle block of Moorlands, the three houses near ours. Mollie and I would love to wander around the village to see which friends we could find to play with. Mollie knew most things happening in Cullingworth - who was ill, born or died. On passing various older village boys they would make the sound of Pathe News music, which made us double up with laughter.

One day Mollie dropped her house door key down the drain. We both stood there perplexed, looking down the drain, which was outside the then fish and chip shop at the bottom of Sun Street.

My grandparents used to live in Sun Street. Then along came the hero of the day, Mr Turner, who was Mollie's next door neighbour. He lifted the drain cover, rolled up his perfectly laundered sleeve and felt about in the filth and found the key, much to Mollie's delight and relief.

I also had a tendency to wander the village on my own, calling to see various friends en route. Kathleen Crabtree (née Blacka) in Mill Street, where we used to spend time sitting on her outside stone steps, leading to nowhere - the door at the top being blocked up!

As I made my way home various villagers would say to me "Your Dad's looking for you all over the village". I would try to get back without being spotted by my very worried father, and had a bit of explaining to do - promising not to do it again. They were wonderful parents, very understanding and allowed me a lovely childhood in Cullingworth.

Dad had a brother, Thomas, a painter and decorator, who lived in Parkside Terrace. I remember when I used to call and play with my cousin and their dog, Uncle Tom was always full of fun, and my aunt would jokingly chide him.

My father's cousin, whom I called Uncle Clifford (Binns), owned the Grocer's shop and his brother Harry at one time owned the Newspaper shop. The latter was a fascinating shop inside and situated a few doors away from Clifford's.

When we went to Clifford's shop he would often have "a new line in biscuits" for us to taste. He put a few on to the tin lid of his biscuit box for us to try. No fancy boxes like you see now, just a silver tin. His sugar was weighed out into bags and tied with a most delightful fine string; very suitable for me to use later for my dolls' house and to make dolls' things.

Uncle Clifford's parents lived at Highfield House, which was a splendid place. Mother used to visit Mrs Binns, known as Auntie Binns to us. We would enter a large sunny airy room, to find the old lady sitting on a chair with a foot stool, wearing a long black dress surrounded by women politely taking tea. I remained very quiet and good, after all little girls were meant to be seen and not heard. Auntie Binns was very used to children though, having lots of her own. I loved visiting there.

HIGHFIELD HOUSE 1920s   Brenda Watering 2004

Highfield House 1920s

I now realise why she had a foot stool - she was a petite lady and I have the same problem, sitting on chairs trying to put my feet on the ground!

Sunday was a day in Church, with mum and Granny. I also attended Chapel which had a schoolroom with a big fire burning. This was near where the new Chapel is now. We used to have teas and games. After Church or Chapel several of us girls would go for a walk down the Woolly Rings or through the fields of wild flowers, gossiping busily together.

Woolly Rings bridge over Cowhouse Beck

When I used to catch the bus in Mill Street which then had very old cottages, now demolished, various locals would inform me that my sister Mildred or brother Kenneth had just left by bus - the time of departure and when they were due to return and where they had gone. Living here in Gayle reminds me of those times.

Although I have a sister and brother they were much older than me - and still are! Mildred 7 years and Kenneth 14 years. They were busy studying for various exams so it was like being an only child for me. Kenneth went away to war in the RAF for many years and father, James Hollings, was in the First World War.

We had our first television set bought for us by Kenneth to keep us company soon after father died in 1953. Kenneth worked in London at the time. He also brought home some Biros which were a very new idea then and somehow had a special smell of plastic. Thinking of plastic, as children we could buy lengths of coloured plastic and would make bracelets for ourselves or to swap. They would be woven into attractive designs.

We used to have a dear old lady living next door to us at Rock House, Mrs Lee. I would regularly visit her and play cards with her and talk and knit. She did some beautiful crochet work, and I still have little dolls' house bags and a small girl's shopping bag and many other lovely items she made for me.

In the wartime, I used to tramp miles with dad to various farms. I loved this. Some farms smelt special - of animal foods cooking. I would follow in dad's footsteps, down long whitewashed passages, with thick tab rugs on the floor and in the parlour would

47

be a huge range with a fire burning and chickens hatching in the hearth. I would sit on a big rocking chair covered in a sheepskin listening to dad talking and drinking tea, soaking up the cosiness of the old farmhouse in candlelight and gaslight. He would fill his pockets with fresh eggs and we would return into the darkness to walk a few miles home again, with our lantern with a candle in it. In winter I had to step into dad's footprints to stop the snow getting into my Wellingtons.

When we arrived home some of the eggs would be stored in water-glass. This was a jelly like substance to preserve the eggs and it was often my job to go down into the cellar to put my little arm into the slime and fish out some eggs for baking with.

On baking day mother made her dough for the bread and put it to rise in front of the fire under a cloth, telling me not to touch it or she would know! After watching it rise for some time, I could not stop myself any longer from prodding the rising dough. Oh what a lovely feeling! The only snag was it showed and the dimple in it got worse when trying to erase it!

Christmas came; cakes were made and out came the copper boiler for pudding cooking. Mother made round Christmas puddings and cooked them in cotton tied at the top and hung into the boiling water from a stick. How delicious they were.

On very cold nights we would have fires lit in our bedroom. Dad would fill up the stone hot water bottles and mum would pile on more blankets. When we didn't have fires lit in the bedrooms, in the morning the windows were so frosted up with the most wonderful designs of icicles, snowflakes and ferns. You could not see out of the window and would breathe onto it to make a little clear patch to peep out of at the snowy world outside.

So many reminiscences to tell, these are just a few of my very happy childhood and friends in Cullingworth.

Brenda Watering

"WE SHALL FIGHT IN THE HILLS"

"There's going to be another War" were the words of my Grandmother as she showed me a picture in the Yorkshire Observer of flag waving crowds in London. I was 5 years old in 1939 and this is the first memory that I can recall of the Second World War.

I have often wondered what fear and sense of foreboding were in the minds of my parents and grandparents at this time. The memories of the horrors of the First World War must have been reawakened. Whatever fears they may have had were not passed on to me, growing up during the War years remains a magical and exciting period of my life.

The first few months of the war appeared to be a preparation for things to come. Gas masks and identity cards were issued. Air Raid Sirens were tested and food was rationed. Ice cream and fruit disappeared from the menu and sweets were in short supply. Food was supplemented by the unloved powdered egg, powdered potato (POM) and Spam.

One morning a line of children were seen being led very slowly down Parkside Terrace. Each child was labelled and carried a gas mask and suitcase. They were evacuees from Bradford. In ones and twos they were being allocated to houses where a spare bedroom was available. Not many of these children were to remain in Cullingworth very long. Most were homesick and returned to Bradford after a few weeks.

Some of the older men together with young men who had not yet reached the age of conscription formed a Home Guard Unit. One of the Home Guard's tasks was, each night, to man a hut at the top of Manywells which served as an outpost to give advance warning of enemy parachutists - it also doubled as a Card School and proved to be so popular that volunteers for night duty were often over-subscribed!

49

Cullingworth Home Guard circa 1940s

A total blackout was introduced. No street lamps were lit and house windows had to be fitted with blackout material. To enforce the blackout came the Air Raid Precaution (ARP) wardens. Their war cry of "put that light out" could be heard during the hours of darkness.

Shortly afterwards, the Auxiliary National Fire Service was formed. They could often be observed attacking imaginary fires in various parts of the village. There was only one recorded fire incident in Cullingworth during the Second World War. This occurred at the National Fire Service's own depot in Mill Street. The fire could not be put out as the water key had been mislaid and so the whole place was gutted!

Now - ready or not - hostilities were about to commence.

At the sound of the first Siren I was unceremoniously dragged from my bed in the middle of the night to huddle with the rest of the family under the bedroom stairs. This, according to the Ministry of Information's instructions was deemed to be the safest area in the house. Here we remained until the "all clear" was sounded. This routine was repeated on the following two or three nights until it was realised that Cullingworth was not going to be Goering's number one target. The threat had receded. Sirens in future were ignored and, I am pleased to say, sleeping arrangements returned to normal.

One night it was Bradford's turn to be bombed. I remember standing at our front door in Brunswick Street and seeing the red sky in the distance and could hear the bombs exploding. We heard the next day that amongst the Luftwaffe's chosen strategic hits was the Odeon Cinema and Lingards Emporium.

As the War progressed, I was aware that the fathers of many of my friends were being conscripted into the Forces. You can imagine my pride and delight when I heard that my own father had received his "Call Up" papers - one look at his face told me that he did not share my enthusiasm for military glory.

With the departure of my father, several of his jobs came my way - attending to the allotment, feeding the hens, collecting the eggs and taking them to the Ministry of Agriculture Packing Station. All egg production, however small, had to be surrendered to the Ministry.

We had no electricity in the house, so the Wireless (Radio) operated with the use of an Accumulator (Battery). The Accumulator had to be taken weekly to Bert Denbigh's hut off Halifax Road, for recharging. The Wireless was our main source of information and entertainment.

The Army arrived one day in the village in the form of a Company of the Royal Army Signals Corps; and overnight Cullingworth became a Garrison Town. The mill in Mill Street was converted into sleeping quarters. The Baptist and Methodist Sunday Schools were requisitioned to become Mess and Drill Halls and the Grange was to be the Officers' Mess.

Camouflaged lorries were parked under the trees at the rear of Parkside Terrace and in Victoria Street. The local children soon realised that the rear of an Army lorry was the ideal hiding place for games of Tin Can Squat (you kicked a can as far as you could, someone then had to go for it whilst the rest hid).

Local villagers provided entertainment for the troops by holding concert parties and dances in the Primary School. Occasionally, the Forces own Entertainment Group (ENSA) would perform in the Baptist School Room. A soldier told me the acronym stood for "Every Night Something Awful"!

Cullingworth was used as a Holding Company by the Army and most personnel were here on a short stay. However, one group stayed longer and many became well known and integrated into village life. After twelve months, it was their turn to go to War. We were to hear later that the whole Company were captured still aboard ship in Singapore Harbour. They spent the rest of the War in captivity under the Japanese.

A Club was formed in the village for boys with an interest in Aircraft. On one of the Spotters Club visits to a nearby airfield, we watched gliders preparing for the "D-Day" landings.

The war was entering its final phase. Eventually "V E Day" arrived, followed by "V J Day". Both celebrated by tea parties and bonfires.

The brutality and full horror of what War could do was brought home to us as we sat in shocked silence when the first Cinema Newsreel pictures of Belson and Hiroshima were shown.

My school friends and I had lived through six years of War unaffected by the major events and had little idea of what peace would bring.

We had indeed been fortunate that home was a small Mill Village tucked away in the Pennines. We had lived almost normal lives away from danger and the turmoil that much of the rest of the world had faced.

Harry Hoult

THE GREAT NORTHERN TRAIL (OPENED 23 MAY 2005)

Fifty years ago the last passenger train ran over Hewenden Viaduct; on May 23 2005 a new footpath and bridleway along the route of the old Great Northern Railway was opened by Cullingworth resident Elsie Hollingsworth, who remembers using the trains from Cullingworth station.

Opening ceremony 23 May 2005

The new Trail is financed by Sustrans, a charity which encourages people to walk, cycle and use public transport, in partnership with other organisations. .

Eventually, the Trail, which starts near the new Primary School, will reach Queensbury at an estimated cost of £1 million. Work on the Thornton section has now started. The Trail crosses Cullingworth Viaduct and the magnificent 150 yards long Hewenden Viaduct, opened in 1882, which curves gently across the valley. Sustrans have provided a number of information boards along the route which give a background to the construction of the railway. Cullingworth History Group is pleased to record a 21st century use for a piece of local history.

John Brigg

AN OPEN LETTER TO THE PEOPLE OF CULLINGWORTH

Landfill Site
Manywells
Cullingworth

10 February 2000

Friends,

As a well established member of the community I would like to take this opportunity to thank everyone who has offered so much support to my family during the past year.

Since the middle of the eighteenth century, my forebears have inhabited this land. They, being descendants of the master race from the Far East, had fallen on hard times during a severe earthquake. These unwelcome guests, had shared this Empire with their nigrescent cousins, who at that time were dramatically declining in numbers as their habitat of timber and clay was being replaced by bricks and mortar. You see, unlike us, they could not adapt to the changing environment. In less than a decade, my forefathers managed to drive out the natives and establish a permanent foothold. The following years were very prosperous; the overcrowded and unsanitary conditions provided the most excellent facilities one could possibly have. However, over a period of time, slum dwellings were increasingly cleared, and substantial improvements were made to sewage systems, thus reducing their main source of food and residence. Ahead lay an even greater threat, caused by the development of chemical warfare, particularly to our species.

Despite these factors, and the threat to our numbers, our long term survival was never at risk.

I have been told by good authority it was in more recent times that my great grandparents first made their acquaintance with Cullingworth. They had enjoyed quite a reasonable standard of living as part of a small colony whose accommodation consisted of a number of farm outbuildings situated about a quarter of a mile south of Milking Hole Beck. The recent milder climate allowed breeding to continue throughout the winter months, which ensured a high survival rate, so it wasn't at all surprising that within the twelve months of 1998, two thousand five hundred descendants evolved from this single pair. Social relationships within the colony had always been harmonious, but as soon as the population density increased dominance structure developed. This meant that high-ranking individuals were taking up favourable positions next to food sources. Excessive pressure was put on those low ranking individuals whose pups had a comparatively low survival rate as they were forced to feed during daylight hours when the dominants were inactive. At this point it became clear that the family was under great pressure because the existing accommodation was both unsafe and inadequate for them, so they started to look further afield for alternatives.

Fortunately, they didn't have far to look - just over the brow there was an open-air palace. After all, what could be better for food, warmth and habitation than a landfill site? Without hesitation great grandfather and his family abandoned the ancestral home to settle in this splendid habitat. The facilities were ideal; fresh food arrived on most days, and regular new arrivals to the family were developing rapidly and well above the national weight and survival rate. By the time I was born the standards of living were higher than one could have dreamed of - a safe home with plenty of food on the doorstep!

Once again, my thanks to the people of Cullingworth and the surrounding area for providing my family and I with such luxury. Truly, it is the equivalent of what I believe humans call "Winning the Lottery".

It is interesting to note that in addition to the benefits outlined above, which are not exclusive to Cullingworth, the recent succession of mild winters has reduced our losses caused by cold, with the result that the rat population has grown to sixty million, the equivalent of one rat for each human in Britain. Yet another reason for us to be grateful to the human race, whose excessive use of fossil fuel is believed to cause global warming, hence the milder winters.

So, thank you humans, on behalf of all the sixty million rodents of Great Britain. Please carry on using your cars instead of taking public transport or walking. Please carry on eating pre-prepared food and throwing half of it away. Through your generosity, I look forward to continuing to live a happy and contented life amongst my harem of females and many thousands of descendants.

Truly yours,

Alpha *Rattus norvegicus*

A REMARKABLE FAMILY

The evolution of Cullingworth throughout the centuries has been greatly complemented by transitory residents who have enriched not only the fabric of the village but also community life. Traces of their presence are to be found in nooks and crannies all around, by the enthusiastic amateur historian. The village has been home to many forward thinking, talented and enterprising individuals who have shaped history not only here but in the wider community. Industrialists, inventors, civil engineers, poets, composers and the ordinary hard working labourer who shaped the landscape have left their mark on the rural community that is inherently Cullingworth.

One such family who resided in and around Cullingworth in the late 18th and early 19th century were the Cravens who originated from Colne. John Craven and his wife Jennett were married in 1768 and had 12 children of whom 9 survived childhood. John was a master stonemason and passed on these skills to his sons. Born in 1780 his sixth son Hiram left Lancashire and moved to Oakworth where he was apprenticed to a stonemason. His first contract was the building of a tiny mill just beyond the Brontë waterfall, between Stanbury and Top Withens. Hiram's interests soon extended to bridge building at a time of increased road construction, which brought him into contact with Joseph Nowell another notable contractor, while engaged on the building of a bridge over the River Nidd at Pateley Bridge. This association was to continue many years with the families further united by marriage. Hiram's son John married Frances the youngest sister of John Nowell and another son Edward, married Mary the only daughter of John.[1]

Hiram had heard of attempts to build a bridge over the River Ouse at York and being undeterred by the earlier failures of others, he contracted for the work. Contractors and engineers before him had been baffled by the swiftly flowing water but Hiram ingeniously devised a way of slowing the current by dropping bales of wool at various points of the river to impede the flow. This enabled him to construct firm foundations to support the great three arched structure which rose 23ft from the river bed. The magnitude of the task was reflected in the 10 years it took to complete the project.

Many of his workmen lived at Hainworth and Oakworth and walked the 40 miles to and from York each week. Begun in February 1810 the bridge was completed in December 1820 at a cost of £50,000 and Hiram was bestowed with the Freedom of the City. His eldest son John continued to work in York as John Craven & Sons and rebuilt most of York Castle walls, worked on several railway contracts and built the docks at Sunderland. The foundation stone was laid on 12 February 1848[2] and the docks and half tide basin were officially opened on 26 June 1850.[3] He lived at Highthorne House, Bishopthorpe York and died there.

In a tiny cemetery known as the Cholera Burying Ground close by the city wall near the railway station, there is a large tombstone which marks the resting place of Hiram's third son who was an architect.

> "Sacred to the memory of Abraham Craven of this City, builder, late of Dockroyd Oakworth, near Keighley, in this County. Third son of Hiram Craven, builder and contractor for the re-erection of the Ouse Bridge, the circumural and public edifices of the Castle of this place. He died of the Asiatic Cholera on Saturday 23 June, Anno Domini, 1832, in his 28th year and was interred the same day, in this then appropriated cemetery.
>
> He like the promising flower that perisheth under the passing storm, was smitten in the bloom of manhood by the unknown pestilence which visited this city, as it traversed its dark path over the earth."

Abraham succumbed to an outbreak so violent that it claimed the lives of 150, who were taken outside the city walls and buried before sunset.

During this time many contracts were completed by Hiram; working with John Nowell on the building of a bridge over the Linlithgow in Scotland;[4] with family members on the construction of aqueducts on the Union Canal, Scotland; East Lancashire Canal; Whitby docks and swing bridge; parts of London and Birmingham railway including the underbridge north of the great embankment and viaduct over the river Ouse in Milton Keynes;[5] York Midland railway and Manchester and Leeds line, including Todmorden tunnel;[6] and nearer home, the building of Wilsden Parish Church and Shipley Parish Church. The road from Oxenhope over Cockhill Moor to Hebden Bridge was the work of the firm and the tiny bridge which carries the road at Oxenhope, whilst miniscule compared to the Ouse Bridge is known to residents as "Hiram's Bridge".[7] The road from Eastburn to Kildwick Bridge was also built by them. His 9th son Edward was killed at Whitby Docks aged 22 in 1833 and Jonas the 8th son died at Fairburn, Ferrybridge in 1839.

Hiram's brother Edward, born 1783 was also trained as a stonemason and his skills were widely used as a contractor of extensive bridge, dock and public works in Hull. Princes Dock built 1825-1829 now extant is attributed to his work.

As the 19th century progressed, both Hiram and Edward also became involved in manufacturing. Hiram had earlier moved to Dockroyd at Oakworth and bought Higher Providence Mill from the Haggas family, putting in two water wheels, one above the other to use the water twice, and constructed a large mill dam. He also built Ebor Mill and rebuilt Providence Mill where two of his sons were engaged in manufacture.[8] Edward came to Cullingworth in 1808 and in partnership with John Haggas took over Ellar Carr Mill. Joseph Harrison had constructed a three storey mill at Ellar Carr in the late 1700s, working both cotton and worsted frames but in the wake of new mechanisation and diminishing trade markets abroad, had failed in 1808 and the mill was auctioned. The manufactory housed 6 spinning frames, 2 for worsted, a picking engine and other equipment powered by water wheel and offered scope for enlargement with the addition of an engine.[9] The availability of coal nearby, sufficient hands from the villages, together with a house and land suggested a viable proposition and Edward Craven and John Haggas leased the mill from the new owner John Greenwood and continued to make cotton goods and yarns until 1816 when they too were bankrupt.[10] Edward Craven then carried on at Ellar Carr in partnership with John Greenwood, whose family had acquired lands at Cowhouse from the Stansfield family of Eshton Hall in 1769.[11] John Greenwood also owned Vale Mill Haworth, Cabbage Mill Keighley, Swarcliffe Mill at Ripon and was in partnership with the Whittakers of Burley at Green Holme Mill. After the death of John Greenwood in 1846 Edward carried on alone constructing the reservoir above the mill, the adjoining cottages and changing from cotton to worsted manufacture. Edward also carried on in his capacity as architect and hydraulic engineer acting for Greenwoods of Keighley, Fosters of Denholme and Townend of Cullingworth.

The lower building adjacent to the cottages housed the warehouse with cottages over, built in 1820

He was also the architect for the Wesleyan Methodist Chapel on Church Street and involved in the planning and building of the

60

Baptist Chapel on Halifax Road, of which he was a Trustee.[12] He moved to Bradford in 1853 and died in 1861 aged 78.

Edward's son Benjamin tenanted 3 houses, a corn mill, stable and reservoir on Mill Street, the croft and Church barn, farmed 26 acres and was listed as corn miller and farmer, continuing until his death in 1882 aged 74.

William Craven, the 7th son of Hiram, born 1803, completed Cold Spring House at Cullingworth in 1835 for his second wife Maria and came to live in the village. He too was a railway contractor and also worsted manufacturer. His second wife Maria was the sister of Jonas Sugden who was in partnership with William's brother Hiram as Craven & Sugden at Higher Providence Mill Oakworth. Maria only enjoyed three years at Cold Spring, dying in 1838. William was a benefactor of the Bingley Wesleyan Methodist Chapel and also Cullingworth Chapel. He died in 1847 aged 44.

Cold Spring House

The prolific Craven family were at the very heart of civil engineering in the first half of the 19th century contracting for Telford, Brunel and Stephenson in the major road, rail and waterway undertakings which remain part of our infrastructure today. Their other enterprises included building public works and churches, soap manufacture, sweet making, rope and sail making, and cotton and worsted manufacturers. Some are mentioned as provisional directors for the making of the Keighley & Worth Valley Railway and others emigrated to Australia where they built Melbourne University.

The descendants of John and Jennet Craven of Colne left lasting testaments to their skills in civil engineering, many of which are still very much in use today, and their associations in business brought them by marriage, into some of the most influential families of the 19th century.

The largest headstone in Colne Parish Church marks the resting place of John, Jennet and 9 of their children. Hiram and Edward Craven are buried in Keighley Parish Churchyard.

Angela Holmes

[1 to 12] *See Bibliography and Notes*

EARLY FLYING MACHINE VISITS CULLINGWORTH

A cold Arctic wind was blowing on the morning of 13 October 1913 when Captain Maclean managed to land his army flying machine on the only level field at Manywells Height. His touchdown at around 7.00 am had been seen by many people living in the area. By 7.30 am when the reporter from the Keighley News arrived there were hundreds of people whose interest had been aroused by the arrival of a flying machine to the misty and bleak hill top.

The hope of all those who braved the chilly breeze was that Captain Maclean would launch his machine once more into the sky. The clouds, however, had now descended over the hill top of Manywells preventing Captain Maclean's departure until there was a marked improvement in the weather.

The crowds, now resigned to a long wait, began to inspect the large flying machine as closely as possible. Two policemen in the crowd kept away anybody who might be tempted to tamper with the machine.

Captain Maclean had experienced an over eager crowd on his first stop at Melton Mowbray when welcoming local residents had placed their autographs on the body of the flying machine. Many people in the crowd at Manywells Height asked the aviator to write his name on all kinds of odd scraps of paper to commemorate his visit to this part of Yorkshire.

As the hours went slowly by and at around 9.30 am the mists showed signs of lifting a little, only to descend again when the wind drove fresh banks of cloud across the sky, blotting out the outlines of the neighbouring hills. Captain Maclean proceeded to don his leather jacket and gave one hopeless glance at the sky as temperatures dropped and the rain began to fall heavily.

It was then decided that any attempt of a flight that day would be useless. Preparations were made for an overnight stay. Starting his machine Captain Maclean taxied across the field to a sheltered corner. Finally, willing hands pushed it into the corner and it was roped to stakes to hold it against the winds.

Hope still lingered in the mind of one elderly lady who hauled a five year old boy in front of the aviator who had by now become thoroughly popular with the crowd due to his unfailing good humour. She asked how much he would want to take the boy for a trip. Promptly, Captain Maclean said "Five Pounds". "Five Pounds" exclaimed the old lady. With a smile the airman said "In other words it isn't allowed". "Go on with ye" said the grand dame "I wouldn't mind givin ye a drink just to take t'little un up". When the Captain showed no signs of wavering she added in a seductive tone "an' a drink us do ye a rare lot o'good this mornin". The Captain whilst agreeing it would be a good idea declined the offer!

From his machine, the aviator produced linen bags, "bed socks" the crowd called them, with which he proceeded to swathe the propeller blades and engine before he left for the weekend as War Office regulations stated that army airmen were not allowed to fly on Sunday. This was the final signal to the crowd that flying was now over for the day and accordingly they went home for dinner.

The army flying machine continued to be the centre of attraction throughout the weekend. The farmer who owned the field put a couple of milk cans near the gate with a notice which read "2 pence for adults, 1 penny for children, admission into the field". Over the weekend thousands of people visited the field from the surrounding villages to see the flying machine.

Captain Maclean's flying machine was a Royal Aircraft Factory BE2A designed by Geoffrey De Havilland. It had a 70hp Renault engine. The BE2A made its first flight on 1 February 1912 and formed the main part of the Royal Flying Corps (RFC) No 2 Squadron which was created on 13 May 1912 and stationed at Farnborough.

No. 2 Squadron received Geoffrey DeHavilland's BE2 as its main aircraft. These frail machines were flown by the Squadron from Farnborough to Montrose in 1913 - no mean feat - and it took them to war in September 1914

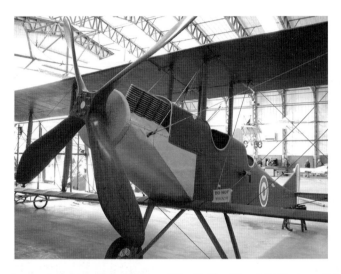

The photographs show the replica of the DeHavilland BE2 aircraft taken at the Elvington Air Museum North Yorkshire

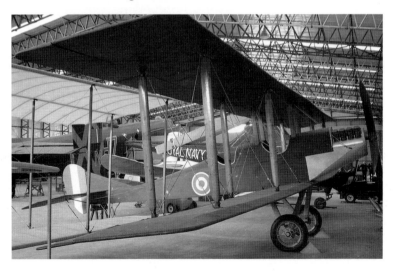

In February 1913 the Squadron moved to Montrose in Scotland, the move taking 13 days. This was the only RFC Unit in Scotland until the outbreak of World War I. On 13 August 1914 the BE2As of No.2 Squadron were the first to arrive and land at Amiens in France. The RFC reconnaissance patrols began over German positions on 19 August 1914 and on 25 August the first German aircraft to be forced down was by three unarmed BE2A aircraft of No. 2 Squadron.

No. 2 Squadron

The BE2A aircraft was the mainstay of the RFC equipping two of the four Squadrons. It was widely used for reconnaissance and artillery spotting in France during the early part of the war.

On Monday 15 October several hundred people witnessed the early arrival of Captain Maclean, who had stayed over the weekend with a friend at Mirfield. He was driven to Manywells by Lt. Ellis, a Territorial Army Officer from Mirfield.

At around 8 am Captain Maclean made a couple of flights around the field to test the flying conditions. On alighting at the end of the second flight the Captain said that the mists were too thick for him to start his journey.

As the morning advanced, and the sun gained height, the mists cleared and at 11.45 am he was able to resume his journey to Montrose. The flying machine took off in a north easterly direction, passing over the village of Harden and St Ives on its flight to Scotland.

Nearly a year later Captain Maclean retraced his flight route back to Farnborough and on to France at the start of World War I.

After the end of the War the new Air Navigation Act was issued on 1 May 1919.

The Air Ministry's 1919 air routes map shows seven new approved main routes for civilian aviation over Great Britain and Ireland. Manywells Height is the end of the route from Hounslow (now Heathrow Airport) via Sheffield.

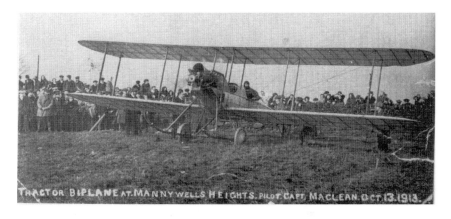

**Captain Maclean and his Flying Machine being pushed into position for his weekend stopover at Manywells Height
13 October 1913**

The general public was apprehensive at the prospect of Civil Flying, a reaction also seen with the coming of the railways and the arrival of the motor car.

Captain Maclean's flight from Farnborough to Montrose in 1913 may well have been a testing of the public's reaction to flying machines passing over their heads.

Great Britain Main Air Routes - under the direction of the Air Ministry the seven main routes, here shown, over Great Britain and to Ireland are now opened for civilian flying

Although Captain Maclean received a friendly reception on his touchdown at Manywells Height, it may have been the unpredictable weather which would affect flying machines that Manywells Height at 271 metres did not become "Leeds Bradford Airport". Instead it was decided that "Yeadon Heights" at only 205 metres would be the site for flying machines to land at the dawn of Civil Aviation.

Derek Goff

68

EXTRACTS FROM THE KEIGHLEY NEWS 1862 - 1918

27th September 1862
Longevity There are now living in Cullingworth and the neighbourhood twenty two persons, all of them of the labouring classes, whose united ages amount to 1,758 years.

1st November 1862
Lecture On Wednesday evening a lecture was delivered to a large and respectable audience in the Baptist Chapel, Cullingworth, by the Rev. M A Wilkinson, Independent Minister of Harden. Mr Thomas occupied the chair. The subject was "The Three Heroes of Babylon". The lecture throughout was full of interest and gave general satisfaction.

6th December 1862
Small Pox This disease and the typhus fever are prevalent in Cullingworth and the neighbourhood. The latter disease has in some cases proved fatal.

1st October 1864
Scarcity of Water During this dry summer water has been very scarce in this neighbourhood; the late rains have had little effect on the springs in consequence of the ground being so very dry, some of them yet scarcely drop into the cisterns. Many people are out of their beds in the morning by three o'clock, going with their cans or pails to the various springs and cisterns to take the water that has dropped during the night.

Last Friday evening, a woman living at Spring Row, being determined to be at the spring first that morning, rose by 2 a.m. and went with her two cans to the cistern where she usually goes to, and in her hurry she forgot a small vessel which she used to have with her to take up the water; but as a woman is very hard to outwit, she actually unloosened the clasp of her clog, and took up by this improvised can, about four gallons which dropped during the night.

The eccentric woman, seeing some of her neighbours going with their pails in the morning, called out to them:

> "Ye noa cashan to goa to yon trough at Loin Side
> cos I wer up at it be tu o'clock, en I forgat me
> lading can, but I tuk watter up i me clog inta me
> cans to mak sur on't"

8th January 1870
Tea Party   On New Year's Day, the Wesleyan Methodists at Hallas Bridge had a public tea party in their schoolroom, which was well attended.

After tea, a public meeting was held in the same place, presided over by Mr John Bailey of Cullingworth. Dialogues and recitations were given by teachers and scholars connected with their school. Mr Joseph Naylor delivered an appropriate address.

5th February 1870
Cullingworth Gate Cow Club   On Monday the annual dinner in connection with this society took place in the afternoon. The members sat down to an excellent dinner at the house of Mr A R Bailey, the Gate Inn. When the cloth was removed Mr J Horsfall was called to the chair and the report for the year read. It showed that there were thirty nine members in the society, and the income for the past year had been £46.11s.3d, and £25.1s.3d had been paid in claims upon the society, leaving a balance in the hands of the treasurer of £21.10s. The officers for the ensuing year were appointed at the meeting.

19th February 1870
Accident   On Thursday afternoon an accident happened to a young man named James Sunderland, of Brown Hill. Sunderland was employed in the combing machine room at Messrs Townend's Mill, and whilst at his work his forefinger on his left hand was caught in the machine and completely taken off by the second joint. He was conveyed to the Bradford Infirmary where he now lies. The young man had only been married about a week.

12th March 1870

Opening of a New Harmonium at Hallas Bridge   On Sunday last, 2 sermons were preached in the Hallas Bridge school room by Mr Joseph Naylor of Cullingworth. The choir of the Cullingworth Wesleyan Chapel sang a selection of anthems.   They were assisted by Miss Hartley of Keighley. At the close of the sermons liberal collections were made which completely defrayed the expense incurred in purchasing the harmonium. On both occasions there was a good attendance.

26th December 1891

Property Development   It is a long time since the village of Cullingworth has been so prosperous as during the past year. It will be remembered that the extensive premises formerly run by Messrs Townend were at a standstill for many years. Last year Messrs J & J Broadbent & Co Ltd of Great Horton acquired the property, and during the present year they have erected a large new wing. They have also erected a new residence for Mr Arthur Craven, a Director of the firm, and about thirty new cottages have been built, with forty more in the course of erection. The quarrying business has also been fairly good. Altogether the prospects of Cullingworth are much brighter than they have been for many years.

27th July 1912

Children's Outing   The popularity of Cullingworth as a pleasant resort is increasing, and a large number of visitors arrive weekly to visit the woods and moors. The Great Horton Church children's service members, to the number of over 300 arrived on Saturday afternoon by a specially chartered train, and after tea visited the various places of interest in the district.   In the evening they assembled at St John's Church, where the service was conducted by Mr Abraham M Drake, who was one of the founders of the children's Sunday evening service in 1876.   Mr W M Castle accompanied the singing on the organ.

12 October 1912

The Property Market   At the George Hotel, Cullingworth, on Monday evening last, Mr Alfred Atkins offered for sale by auction six dwelling houses situate at Cow House Bridge, Cullingworth. Bidding commenced at £100 and rose to £143, at which figure they were sold to Mr William Whittaker, coal merchant, Cullingworth.

2nd November 1912
The Property Market   On Tuesday evening last, Messrs Ackroyd and Sons offered for sale by auction at the Fleece Hotel, Cullingworth, six cottages in Lodge & Mill Street, Cullingworth, which were sold for £190; and four cottages, house and shop and stable situate at Cullingworth Gate, which were sold for £240. Both lots were purchased by Mr George Meakin.   There was a good attendance and some spirited bidding.   Messrs Wright and Wright, Keighley, were the solicitors for the vendors.

4th July 1914
Garden Party at Hallas Hall   In connection with the Cullingworth Parish Church a very successful and enjoyable garden party was held in the Hallas Hall grounds, Cullingworth on Saturday last on the invitation of Mr and Mrs Arthur Craven.   The Keighley YMCA Orchestral Band rendered selections afternoon and evening, and tea was provided on the lawn. Lawn tennis, croquet, rifle shooting, archery and golf were played.   The Knowle field was lent by Mr George Bailey, and from here the gathering had a splendid view of Bingley, Baildon, Rombalds Moor and the Harden Valley. The proceeds were given to the organ repair fund.

7th November 1914
Garments for soldiers   In association with the Cullingworth branch of the Red Cross Society the following articles have been forwarded to the Society during the last few weeks: 55 night-shirts, 10 day-shirts, 11 flannel bed-jackets, 37 handkerchief, 30 mufflers, 15 pairs woollen cuffs, 150 bandages, 12 pillow cases, 3 helmets, 5 pairs of gloves, 36 pairs socks, 5 pairs bed-socks, also cigarettes, notepaper and postcards.   Working meetings have been held at Hallas Lodge, kindly lent by Mrs A Craven, who generously gave the materials for the first consignment.   A house to house collection for the same object realised £17.15s. Altogether 463 garments have been made and forwarded.

13th February 1915
Cigarettes for soldiers   The members of the YMCA at Cullingworth have collected and sent 1,700 cigarettes to soldiers who have gone to the front from the village.   Letters have been received expressing thanks for the cigarettes and appealing for further gifts of a similar nature.

22nd May 1915
Eggs for the wounded   Last week 368 eggs were collected in Cullingworth for the wounded soldiers and sailors. Of these 100 were taken to the Military Hospital in Keighley and the remainder have been sent to London.

20th April 1918
Railway Memorabilia   Mr George Woodiwiss has made a gift of forty-nine volumes on railway engineering to the Bingley District Council's Free Library and the Clerk to the council was instructed on Monday evening to convey the thanks of the Council to Mr Woodiwiss.

26th October 1918
Influenza   Owing to the prevalence of influenza the medical officer has closed the Cullingworth day schools until Monday, November 4th. A great many adults as well as children are suffering from this complaint.

9th November 1918
The future   To repair the damage of the Great War it will be necessary for the next generation to be trained in all that makes for greatness - sobriety, thrift, high moral character. All these are represented in the training given to the members of the Independent Order of Rechabites. Let your children have the advantage of this training by becoming members of the Juvenile Section. Full particulars can be obtained from Mr S Peacock, 21 Roydwood Terr. and Mr J E Jowett, Woodview, Cullingworth.
(This was an advertisement)

Diana Tottle

CULLINGWORTH POST OFFICE SAGA

The following is an article which appeared in the *Keighley News* on the 3 May 1862 concerning the local Post Office:

"Considerable inconvenience is felt by the inhabitants of Cullingworth in consequence of the non-central position of the village Post Office. The Post Office at present is situate at Cullingworth Gate, a quarter of a mile from the bulk of the houses, and some of the inhabitants more public-spirited than the rest, called a meeting to try what could be done towards having the office removed. A party, however, exists actuated perhaps by sympathy with the present post-mistress and reluctance to remove her from her post, who oppose any change in the matter. The first meeting was adjourned, owing to an alleged informality in the convening of it, and a second was held last week in the Oddfellows' Hall, on the subject. An official visitor from Leeds had, it seems, in the meantime been to the place, and, it is said, expressed his opinion that no change need be made. Not deterred by this, a committee was, however, formed, determined to try what could be done towards the remedy of what they consider a crying evil, and at all events, resolved to agitate the question till some good comes of it. The reason of the office being originally placed so far from the village, appears to be that the postman who then passed from Bradford to Haworth should not lose time in going out of his way. Now, however, he goes through the village, and that reason therefore has ceased to exist."

A further article concerning the Post Office, addressed to the Editor of the *Keighley News* appeared in the paper on 24 May 1862

Sir, In a paragraph in the *Keighley Guardian* on 10 May, there is an attempt made to defend the part taken by the Reverend J H Mitchell, incumbent of Cullingworth, with reference to the removal of the Post Office from Cullingworth Gate to Cullingworth. The writer refers to a meeting held for that purpose on the 15 ult. As I was present at that meeting I will give a few details. The meeting which was posted in the public places in the village, and lest Mr Mitchell (who lived at some distance) might not be appraised of it, a letter was sent to him by special messenger. We did not anticipate any opposition (except from a few who reside in the immediate vicinity of the post office) least of all from Mr Mitchell himself, who during a previous agitation had been in favour of its removal.

But Mr Mitchell's views for some reason have undergone a change, and no sooner did he learn what was the object of the meeting that he came down to the village, collected his party and brought them down to the meeting to oppose us. He was called to the chair and he spent nearly the whole time in protesting against the meeting, denouncing it as illegal, on the ground that it was not in the church vestry, and that full three weeks' notice had not been posted up. We were further told that were we to carry out our point he could get the whole matter reversed, owing to the illegality of the meeting. One of the opposition party, on being asked by the chairman if he had not had a proposition to make, rose and proposed an adjournment of the meeting for the following week, as the present meeting was illegal. It was to be held in the church vestry. The chairman actually put the proposition to the meeting, and gave it his sanction, although he had just stated that no meeting of that kind could be legal unless a public notice had been posted up for three full weeks. Where is the consistency in this? The general impression is that the rigmarole about the church vestry and the full three weeks' notice was all a delusion, and resorted to in order to gain time.

In the paragraph alluded to, we are accused of violating "principles of honour, good faith" etc. But where were the "principles of honour, good faith" etc of Mr Mitchell and his party, when after having proposed the adjournment of the meeting to the church vestry, when the hour arrived kept the doors locked against us? But it is said that, owing to the visit of the surveyor, who decided against its removal, Mr M and everyone else were released from either calling or attending any further meeting upon the question. But we should have thought that their "principles of honour, good faith" would have led them to do one of two things – either (first) to give public notice that owing to the visit of the surveyor there existed no longer any necessity for such meeting; or (second) to have attended the meeting and inform the public of what had been done.

The paragraph further states that it was decided that there was no ground for its removal. But what would they consider sufficient ground for removal? To all sensible men there seems sufficient ground for removal when:

1   the Post Office is nearly half a mile from the great bulk of the inhabitants; and

2   when nearly the whole of the Cullingworth letters, instead of passing through the Cullingworth Post Office, are left at different private houses in the village, to be taken up by the postman as he passes through from Denholme.

The paragraph also states that the meeting was summoned to be held in the Parish Church, we beg to say that the Parish Church is not at Cullingworth but at Bingley, three miles distant.

Yours etc

ONE OF THE ACCUSED"

Marjorie Holland

NEW CONSERVATIVE CLUB AT CULLINGWORTH

The opening ceremony of the new Conservative Club in Cullingworth was reported in the 28th November 1891 edition of the *Keighley News* and an extract of the article follows:

"On Saturday evening a new Conservative Club in Towngate, Cullingworth, was opened to the members, of whom there are between seventy and eighty, by Mr. F. S. Powell, M.P., an extensive landowner in the district.

The club has been provided and fitted up by Mr. Powell, from whom the committee have leased the premises. They consist of what were formerly three cottages, the interior of which have been gutted and completely rearranged. They include a spacious billiard-room with a spectators' gallery, a smoke-room, a recreation-room, a reading-room, two committee-rooms, a bath-room, and accommodation for a curator. The rooms are very neatly decorated and well fitted, and are in every respect highly suitable for the purpose to which they are to be devoted.

The first event of the day was the presentation of an address to Mr. Powell on behalf of his tenants, several of whom met him at the George Hotel. The Rev. T. Mellody [vicar of Cullingworth] opened the proceedings. The address, which was read by Mr. A. L. Hill, and presented by Mr. Henry Moulding, the oldest tenant, spoke of the large sums of money which Mr.Powell had spent upon the tenants' holdings during the last twenty years, which sums had been a considerable boon to them during a period of extreme depression.

(Mr Powell's response then follows in the article).

Subsequently a gold key was presented to Mr. Powell on behalf of the members of the club by Mr. E. Greenwood."

Cullingworth Conservative Club (centre of the picture) circa 1930s

The following is an extract from 'Sir Francis Sharp Powell: a Memoir by his nephew' written by Henry L P. Hulbert and published by Richard Jackson in 1914 concerning the opening of the new Conservative Club in the village:

"Mr. Powell made himself personally acquainted with his tenants and their needs, in which he took the most kindly and practical interest. His kindness and consideration as a landlord were fully appreciated. In November 1891, his tenants at Cullingworth presented him with an illuminated address, expressed in most affectionate terms, on the occasion of the opening of the new Conservative Club in the village. The members of the old Conservative Club had received notice to quit and Mr. Powell stepped into the breach and converted some of his cottage property at Towngate, Cullingworth, into a club for them."

Helen Marshall

MEMORIES OF A CULLINGWORTH HARDWARE SHOP

In recent times in order to expand its premises "Cullingworth Stores" situated on Halifax Road took over a hardware shop.

When I was small, in the 1940s, up to the 1960s, the small hardware shop was owned by Miss Annie Ackroyd, who at that time sold virtually everything you might need. The shop had small drawers from floor to ceiling, and sold bolts for old carriages, fretsaw blades, nails and screws for every eventuality, as well as baking tins, pans, paraffin, black leading and even gas mantles. Miss Ackroyd was even known to ask Kathleen Crabtree, née Blacka, if she would bring her a large bag of nails from the shop where she worked in Keighley, as she was running short. It was also reputed that she had the first bath installed and villagers paid to have a bath, probably 1p or so at that time. She was a very enterprising lady, and a staunch Baptist.

After she died the business was taken over by the local plumber, Kenneth Hird, who revamped the upstairs into living accommodation. His mother-in-law, Mrs Spencer, ran the shop with occasional help from his wife. The local electrician used the cellar for storage.

When the shop was again sold, the electricians, Laycock Bros took over the whole lot, and I helped to run the hardware part with assistance from my sister-in-law. By now the shop sold the odd dinner service, vases, fancy type bits and pieces, calor gas and gardening equipment as well as the nuts, bolts, screws and paraffin etc. This would be around the middle of the 1970s to 1980s.

During this time, "Wharton's Watch and Clock" moved their business from the premises across the road into the back room of the shop.

Bill Laycock, the electrician, died very suddenly and his partner had no wish to carry on with the shop which was then sold to "Cullingworth Stores", and 'Wharton's Watch and Clock" business returned to its original premises across the road, wedged between a house on one side and a butchers shop on the other. At the time of writing this article the premises are now occupied by "Hair Flair" and the adjoining "house" is vacant following the closure of "Rachel's Flowers".

Janet Wharton

FARMING TALES - EXTRACTS FROM KEIGHLEY NEWS 1862

5th July 1862
<u>Fatal Accident to a Pig</u> A man named Matthew Wade of Cullingworth, having purchased two pigs at Halifax fair on Saturday for £4.12s was returning home with the animals in the afternoon when one of the two, apparently dissatisfied with leaving its companions in Halifax was difficult to drive. With the obstinacy for which the porcine tribe is famous "Piggy" made desperate efforts to return from whence it came and in doing so unfortunately got under the wheels of a loaded wagon, was run over, and killed on the spot.

16th August 1862
<u>Extraordinary Hen</u> A few days ago a hen, the property of Mr James Farrar of Denholme laid 4 eggs in 24 hours, all perfectly shelled and measuring 3½ inches in length by 6½ inches in circumference. About a week ago the same hen laid 2 eggs in one day. She is of Malay and Spanish breed.

Derek Goff

BIBLIOGRAPHY AND NOTES

A LOCAL FEUD: LANDOWNER VS MILL OWNER
Footnote [1]: Possibly an independent building on the main Cullingworth Mills site
Footnote [2]: From *Ancient Bingley*, J Horsfall Turner, published 1897
Footnote [3]: Courtesy of Bradford Reference Library

Diaries of W B Ferrand, 1861-1867
B.P.P. Inquiry into the Pollution of the Rivers Aire and Calder 1867
Keighley News 1866

FAIRFAX IN THE FIFTIES
Personal reflections
Photographs courtesy of Betty Crabtree

THOMAS WHITTLE - FIRST HEADMASTER OF CULLINGWORTH BOARD SCHOOL
Cullingworth Board School Log Book 1880-1904
Preliminary Statement, Cullingworth Board School, June 1882
Cullingworth Joint Board School committee meetings minute book 1881-1903
Bingley School Board minute book 1878-1886

"THISTLE" WEDDING DRESS
Photographs taken by Derek Goff by kind permission of Liz McIvor, Curator of Bolling Hall Museum

HOW DID I GET MIXED UP IN ALL THIS?
Personal reflections
Photograph of work party taken by Pat Goff

A SHORT HISTORY OF CULLINGWORTH VILLAGE HALL
Personal reflections
Footnote [1]: Over 60s Club Table Cloth Names List 1967 compiled for the Cullingworth History Group 2005 by members Steve and Beryl Tickle
Plans and photographs courtesy of the Village Hall Committee
Isometric projection, David L Steel, Building Services Bingley

MEMORIES OF THE BAPTIST CHAPEL
Personal reflections
Photographs courtesy of Harry Hoult

REMINISCENCES OF LIFE IN CULLINGWORTH BEFORE 1955
Personal recollections
Ink drawings by Brenda Watering
Photograph courtesy of Harry Hoult

"WE SHALL FIGHT IN THE HILLS"
"We shall fight in the Hills" quotation Winston Churchill June 1940
A villager's recollections of the War Years in Cullingworth

THE GREAT NORTHERN TRAIL (OPENED 23 MAY 2005)
Personal reflections
Photograph taken by Derek Goff

AN OPEN LETTER TO THE PEOPLE OF CULLINGWORTH
A thank you letter from a grateful resident. The author is indebted to Jane Breen for providing factual information

A REMARKABLE FAMILY
Footnotes:

[1] Frederick Nowell *The Nowells* 1909 reprinted from the *Dewsbury Reporter* 30 July 1932 P2

[2] *Illustrated News* P83 12/2/48

[3] *Railway Times* P640 29/6/50

[4] *The Nowells* P2

[5] M Barnes PhD.BSc C/Mgt FCIOB, FICE, FREng *Civil Engineering management in the Industrial Revolution* 2000 Paper 12109 P140

[6] *Todmorden History*

[7] N C Whitehead (Great grandson of Hiram) compiler of family history. Keighley Reference Library

[8] J Hodgson *Textile Manufacture and other Industries* 1879 P154

[9] *Halifax Journal* 13 August 1808 West Yorkshire Archaeology Service

[10] *Leeds Intelligencier,* 6 May 1816 West Yorkshire Archaeology Service

[11] *Bardsley Powell Colln,* Box 36 Sheepscar Archives Leeds, now at Bradford Archives

[12] *Cullingworth Baptist Records,* Wakefield County archives Ref C422

Other sources:
The author is indebted to Mr F Smith of Bolton who kindly passed on correspondence from Mr N Whitehead
Photographs taken by P Holmes 1985

EARLY FLYING MACHINE VISITS CULLINGWORTH
Illustrated Encyclopaedia of Aviation Volumes 12, 14 & 16
Photographs of BE2 taken by Derek Goff
Keighley News 13 October 1913
The New Illustrated 10 May 1919 - courtesy of Kenneth Kenzie

CULLINGWORTH POST OFFICE SAGA
Keighley News, 3 May 1862 and 24 May 1862

NEW CONSERVATIVE CLUB AT CULLINGWORTH
Keighley News, 28 November 1891
Sir Francis Sharp Powell: a Memoir by his nephew, Henry L P. Hulbert, published by Richard Jackson, 1914

MEMORIES OF A CULLINGWORTH HARDWARE SHOP
Personal reflections